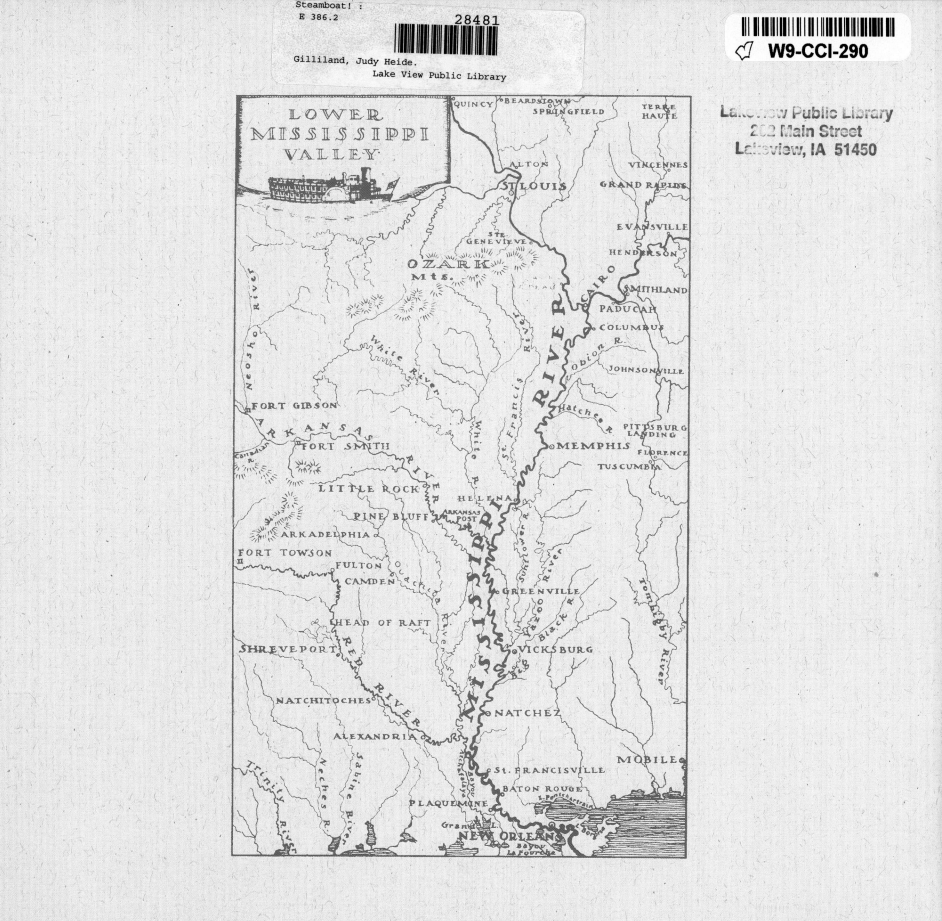

LOWER
MISSISSIPPI
VALLEY

In loving memory of Penny Gilliland
J. H. G.

Acknowledgments

For their generous help in researching this book, we would like to thank Captain Clarke Campbell Hawley, former captain of the *Natchez IX*, New Orleans; Pamela D. Arceneaux, The Historic New Orleans Collection, Williams Research Center; Ann E. Smith Case, University Archives, Tulane University Library; and Michele Vitti Lawton. We would also like to thank Genelle Hunter Bauer-Scott for allowing us to include the map by Isabella Brockway Walker that originally appeared in *Steamboats on the Western Rivers*, by Louis C. Hunter, published by Harvard University Press.

A Melanie Kroupa Book

DK
Ink

Dorling Kindersley Publishing, Inc.,
95 Madison Avenue, New York, New York 10016

Visit us on the World Wide Web at http://www.dk.com

Text copyright © 2000 Judith Heide Gilliland
Illustrations copyright © 2000 Holly Meade

Photo of Captain Blanche Leathers on page 37 courtesy of the Louisiana Collection, Howard Tilton Memorial Library, Tulane University.

Dorling Kindersley Publishing offers special discounts for bulk purchases for sales promotions or premiums. Specific large-quantity needs can be met with special editions, including personalized covers, excerpts of existing guides, and corporate imprints. For more information, contact Special Markets Dept., Dorling Kindersley Publishing, Inc., 95 Madison Ave., New York, NY 10016; fax: (800) 600-9098.

Library of Congress Cataloging-in-Publication Data

Gilliland, Judith Heide.
    Steamboat! the story of Captain Blanche Leathers / by Judith Heide Gilliland;
illustrated by Holly Meade — 1st ed.
            p.   cm.
    "A Melanie Kroupa book"
    Summary: Describes how Blanche Douglas Leathers studied the Mississippi River and passed the test to become a steamboat captain in 1894.
    ISBN 0-7894-2585-8
    1. Leathers, Blanche—Juvenile literature. 2. Women ship captains—Mississippi River—Biography—Juvenile literature. 3. Paddle steamers—Mississippi River—Juvenile literature. [1. Leathers, Blanche. 2. Sailors. 3. Women—Biography.] I. Meade, Holly, ill. II. Title.
    VK140.L34G55   2000
    386'.224'092—dc21   99-14811
    [B]   CIP

The illustrations for this book were created with cut paper and paint.
Book design by Chris Hammill Paul. The text of this book is set in 16 point Cochin.

Printed and bound in U.S.A.
First Edition, 2000

2 4 6 8 10 9 7 5 3 1

STEAMBOAT!

The Story of Captain Blanche Leathers

Judith Heide Gilliland

pictures by Holly Meade

Dorling Kindersley Publishing, Inc.

BLANCHE DOUGLAS sits on the riverbank and listens to the sounds of the Mississippi River. It is 1868, and she is eight years old.

Some days the river is a wild place. It rages like an ocean in a storm. Some days it is a foggy phantom and Blanche can hardly see it. But always she can hear it.

Today the river is a lake—still, smooth, and sleepy. The muddy waters whisper a quiet secret.

Blanche knows the secret: that the river is *never* still, smooth, and sleepy. Not underneath.

Underneath and invisible is the channel, a river inside the river. Always it runs swiftly, silently, dangerously. On days like this, the river is a trickster, pretending to be daydreaming but really wide awake.

Blanche loves the river, calm or wild. It is never the same, it always changes. Nothing humdrum about it!

Today she will be the first to see the smoke of the steamboat as it nears the landing.

There it is! A puff of cloud! "Steamboat ahoy!" shouts Blanche. A whistle screams, and birds fly from the trees. Blanche knows all of the steamboats and each of their whistles. She can tell by the sound that it is the *J. P. Whittaker*.

And here it comes, grand and white, gleaming in the sun:

STEAMBOAT! Big and tall, a floating birthday cake. It looks like a celebration. The paddle wheel turns and drips water, flames glow in the furnace, smoke rolls out of the smokestacks.

There is Captain Blackstone, standing tall in the pilot house. "Tie her up, men! And don't be all day about it!" he bellows.

A crowd gathers from the plantation to see what the *J. P. Whittaker* brings: mail from upriver, and news. Maple syrup for Harwood's General Store; a pony for Harriet Bannister. And Mr. Parson's grand piano. Hustle and bustle to a slow, hot day.

Everyone watches the roustabouts heave loads of cotton bound for New Orleans onto the deck. There is so much cotton today that it reaches as high as the pilot house.

"How do you do, Mr. Blackstone?" Blanche's father, Mr. Douglas, has come to see that the cotton from his plantation is loaded safely onto the *J. P. Whittaker.* "How is the river today?"

Mr. Blackstone is solemn. "Passing fair, she is now," he growls, "but last night the fog was so thick you could hear it." The crowd leans closer to listen. "Why, I heard a hundred ghost steamboats moaning and calling out warnings, and"—he lowers his voice—"I spied something glowing under the water."

Everyone shivers.

The river has another secret: It is a graveyard, a steamboat graveyard, and the bones of sunken boats lie below. Some have gone down in storms, some have gone up in explosions, but most have been trapped by what lies beneath the surface.

Everybody knows that being a steamboatman requires daring and intelligence.
Nobody knows that Blanche has decided to be a steamboatman when she grows up.

It is 1872, and Blanche is twelve years old.
Mr. Blackstone and Mr. Douglas talk about
the recent steamboat explosion. "Blew off
both smokestacks and sent the whole
boat flying sky-high, I hear," growls
Mr. Blackstone. "Steamboats aren't
meant to fly."

Blanche is listening. She smiles. "I am
going to be a steamboat captain someday,"
she announces.

Mr. Blackstone raises his big eyebrows.
And then he laughs. "Girls don't grow up
to be steamboatmen," he replies.

It is 1876, and Blanche is sixteen years old. It is night, and she is listening to the thunder. Rain and wind rattle the house as lightning cracks down the sky. Over all the noise, Blanche can hear a steamboat whistle calling. She wishes she were on board.

It is 1881, and Blanche is a young woman now. She meets a handsome young steamboat captain. His name is Captain Bowling Leathers, and the name of his steamboat is the *Natchez*. It is the grandest and fastest steamboat on the Mississippi. Love at first sight!

Mr. Leathers and Blanche Douglas marry.

"Welcome to the *Natchez*, my dear," says Mr. Leathers. "I hope you don't mind living on a steamboat!"

Everything on the boat is handsome and grand. Silver teapots and gleaming brass and thick carpets. There is music every night, there are elegant dinners. Presidents and princes travel on board the *Natchez*. "Charming lady!" they say about Blanche. "Like an angel!" they all agree. There is much merriment and laughter.

But Blanche feels the river beneath her feet. She has not forgotten her dream.

Late one night Blanche hears the steamboat whistle high above her, calling out to the night, calling out to her.

She climbs out of bed and joins her husband in the pilot house, far above the music and laughter. Up here the river is everything.

"How can you know where you're going?" Blanche asks her husband. All she can see is blackness and shadow, strange ghostly shapes.

"I know the river. I know that over there in the dark is an island, and that just ahead, the night hides a fallen tree. And that light in the distance — that's a signal lantern on Joe Green's landing. He must have some cotton for us to pick up."

Blanche peers out at the night.

Captain Leathers says, "The river is like a book. Captains who don't read carefully lose their boats and their passengers to the muddy waters."

Blanche looks steadily at her husband. Then she says, "I want to learn the river."

NAT

And so, day after day, night after night, Blanche stands at the wheel next to her husband and studies, watches, and learns the language of the river.

A dimple in the water: That means BEWARE, a sunken wreck awaits, ready to tear out the bottom of a steamboat!

A faint shadow: That means WATCH OUT, a sandbar lurks below, waiting to capture any boat that strays too near!

A dark spot: DANGER, a lost island lies beneath the surface, fishing for steamboats!

And every day the river rises and falls, making new loops and cutting off old ones, sweeping away riverbanks and trees.

Blanche studies hard. She rubs her eyes
and stares at her maps. "I can learn this —
I *will* learn this," she says.
　　It is the hardest thing she has ever done.

Finally Blanche knows the Mississippi. She
knows it going up (which is one thing) and going down
(which is another thing altogether). She knows it in
daylight and in moonlight. She knows it in still and
in storm.

One day Blanche says to her husband,
"I want to be a steamboat captain."
　　He looks at her in surprise. Then he replies,
"And a very good captain you would make, too!"

To become a captain, Blanche must go to New Orleans and pass a difficult exam. One of the examiners is Mr. Blackstone, whose big eyebrows are now white. He raises them as high as they will go, and they stay there when he learns that Blanche means to become a steamboat captain.

The examiners look at Blanche, and then they look at one another. This is unheard of: a steamboatwoman. The exam must surely be too difficult for a woman.

Mr. Blackstone asks the first question. "Can you describe the Mississippi River from Potter's plantation to Blake's plantation, upstream?"

Blanche replies, "I know it well. It is a
stretch of fifty miles, south of Vicksburg."
She describes the trees,
          the rocks,
    the bushes,   the snags,
            the banks,
        the bluff reefs,
    the houses on the banks,
                the landings,
  the island that lies one hundred
and thirty yards east of the tupelo tree
        with the split trunk,
    the depth of the water on Tuesday.

For a long time the examiners
question Blanche, and now all of them
        are surprised. There is only one
        thing left to do. "Tonight we will
        test your navigational skills on the
        Natchez," says Mr. Blackstone.

That night Blanche welcomes the examiners to the steamboat. She serves them tea in the pilot house. "Shall we begin?" she suggests politely. It is a starless, moonless night, black as ink. It will be a difficult test indeed.

From one side of the river to the other, Blanche pilots the steamboat around snags and rocks, through shadows that look like boulders, and over water that looks like solid ground.

All is smooth sailing, until . . . a soft scrape, a warning. The examiners look at one another uneasily. They are pilots themselves. They know what that sound means:

SANDBAR! A word that strikes fear into the hearts of all captains. It can grab the steamboat like a toy, capsize it . . . or even sink it. No doubt Blanche Leathers will try to back away, or stop the engines altogether. The examiners brace themselves. Blanche is calm. "Full steam, Henry." She talks to the engine room through the speaking tube. "All the power she has, please."

They are going forward, straight into the sandbar!

There is a rush of paddles and sand, of water and loud heartbeats.

The steamboat rises! For a moment, it seems to fly. The huge sternwheeler, with its staterooms and ballrooms and dining rooms, with its three decks and two chimneys and fiery boilers, lifts up a little, and up a little more . . .

. . . and then over.
The sandbar is behind them!
   "Nice and easy now, Henry,"
says Blanche.
   Then all is quiet.

The steamboat resumes its journey.
   "More tea, gentlemen?" Blanche asks.
   "Fine piloting," says Mr. Blackstone. "Fine piloting indeed."
His teacup rattles in his hand. His eyebrows quiver. "In fact,
some of the finest piloting I have ever seen."
   Blanche has passed her exam with high honors.

It does not take long for all of New Orleans to hear the news: It is 1894, and Blanche Leathers is a steamboat captain!

This calls for a celebration, something New Orleans is very good at.

There are five hundred passengers on the *Natchez*, famous actors and gamblers, politicians and plantation owners, and Mr. Blackstone, too.

Tugboats, pleasure boats, steamboats, and rafts follow Captain Blanche Leathers on her maiden voyage up the Mississippi. They blow their whistles and sound their horns.

From New Orleans to Vicksburg, well-wishers line the banks, cheering.

It is so noisy, hardly anyone can hear the river today. But Blanche can.
She looks at the crowds. Then she takes something out of her pocket
and glances at it. It is her new business card.

THE STEAMBOAT NATCHEZ

YES,
I AM A STEAMBOATMAN

Captain Blanche Leathers

In the nineteenth century the Mississippi River was like a grand highway, and the king of the road was the steamboat. Steamboats lined the levee at New Orleans for a stretch of five miles, a forest of smokestacks as far as the eye could see. They carried everything—passengers, produce, and manufactured goods—and provided the main means of communication from New Orleans to Vicksburg . . . to Memphis . . . to St. Louis, all the way north to Minneapolis.

Blanche Douglas was born in 1860 and grew up during the heyday of steamboating, when a job on one of these floating palaces was the dream of boys everywhere. In Blanche's day, captains were men. And the average steamboat lasted only five years before the river claimed it. But that wasn't about to stop Blanche. She was determined to pilot a steamboat, and she did.

Her kindness, as well as her skill, became legend on the river, and she was called the "Angel of the Mississippi." Newspapers and magazines of the time celebrated Blanche's success and published many interviews with the "Little Captain." She said, "The river is like a person. It has character, judgment, charm. You must learn to read the face of the water like a book, learn the meaning of every ripple, every shadow. You must know every inch of the river so accurately that you will not be deceived by fogs that magnify objects . . . or moonlight that throws deceptive shadows . . . or darkness that makes the bank of the river look ten feet higher."

The steamboat's days of glory were numbered. The first decade of the twentieth century saw the railroad become all-powerful. Now the locomotive was king. But Blanche understood change. She told a reporter, "Today belongs to land. Tomorrow—air. That is life, nothing humdrum about it. I love it!"

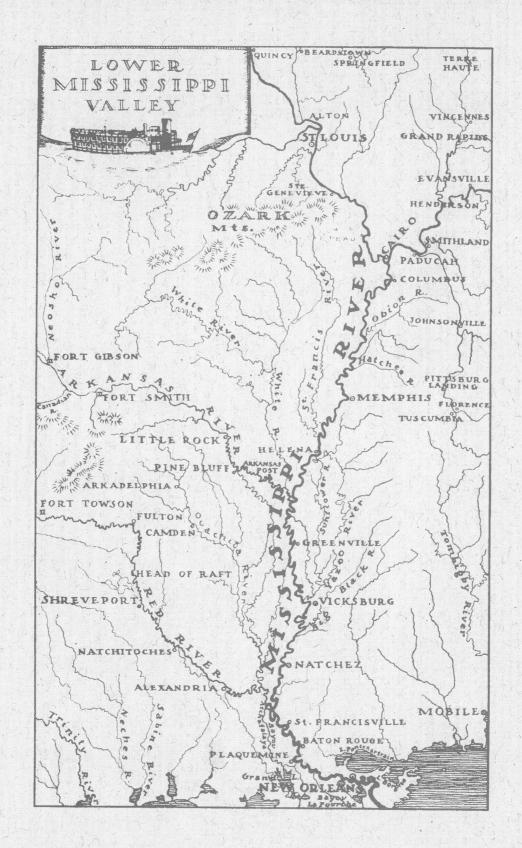